Population Estimates for the Toiyabe Population of the Columbia Spotted Frog (*Rana luteiventris*), 2004–10

By Michael J. Adams, U.S. Geological Survey; Chad Mellison, U.S. Fish and Wildlife Service; and Stephanie K. Galvan, U.S. Geological Survey

Prepared in cooperation with the U.S. Fish and Wildlife Service (Region 8) and the Nevada Natural Heritage Program

Open-File Report 2013–1036

U.S. Department of the Interior
U.S. Geological Survey

U.S. Department of the Interior
KEN SALAZAR, Secretary

U.S. Geological Survey
Marcia K. McNutt, Director

U.S. Geological Survey, Reston, Virginia: 2013

For more information on the USGS—the Federal source for science about the Earth,
its natural and living resources, natural hazards, and the environment—visit
http://www.usgs.gov or call 1–888–ASK–USGS

For an overview of USGS information products, including maps, imagery, and publications,
visit *http://www.usgs.gov/pubprod*

To order this and other USGS information products, visit *http://store.usgs.gov*

Suggested citation:
Adams, M.J., Mellison, C., and Galvan, S.K., 2013, Population estimates for the Toiyabe population of the Columbia spotted frog (*Rana luteiventris*), 2004–10: U.S. Geological Survey Open-File Report 2013-1036, 30 p.

Contents

Figures

Tables

Conversion Factors

Multiply	By	To obtain
	Length	
inch (in.)	2.54	centimeter (cm)
inch (in.)	25.4	millimeter (mm)
foot (ft)	0.3048	meter (m)
mile (mi)	1.609	kilometer (km)
mile, nautical (nmi)	1.852	kilometer (km)
yard (yd)	0.9144	meter (m)

Population Estimates for the Toiyabe Population of the Columbia Spotted Frog *(Rana luteiventris)*, 2004–10

By Michael J. Adams, U.S. Geological Survey; Chad Mellison, U.S. Fish and Wildlife Service; and Stephanie K. Galvan, U.S. Geological Survey

Introduction

The Toiyabe population of Columbia spotted frogs (*Rana luteiventris*, hereafter "Toiyabe frogs") is a geographically isolated population located in central Nevada (fig. 1). The Toiyabe population is part of the Great Basin Distinct Population Segment of Columbia spotted frogs, and is a candidate for listing under the Endangered Species Act (U.S. Fish and Wildlife Service, 2011). The cluster of breeding sites in central Nevada represents the southernmost extremity of the Columbia spotted frogs' known range (Funk and others, 2008).

Toiyabe frogs are known to occur in seven drainages in Nye County, Nevada: Reese River, Cow Canyon Creek, Ledbetter Canyon Creek, Cloverdale Creek, Stewart Creek, Illinois Creek, and Indian Valley Creek. Most of the Toiyabe frog population resides in the Reese River, Indian Valley Creek, and Cloverdale Creek drainages (fig. 1; Nevada Department of Wildlife, 2003).

Approximately 90 percent of the Toiyabe frogs' habitat is on public land. Most of the public land habitat (95 percent) is managed by the U.S. Forest Service (USFS), while the Bureau of Land Management (BLM) manages the remainder. Additional Toiyabe frog habitat is under Yomba Shoshone Tribal management and in private ownership (Nevada Department of Wildlife, 2003).

The BLM, USFS, Nevada Department of Wildlife (NDOW), Nevada Natural Heritage Program (NNHP), Nye County, and U.S Fish and Wildlife Service (USFWS) have monitored the Toiyabe population since 2004 using mark and recapture surveys (Nevada Department of Wildlife, 2004). The USFWS contracted with the U.S. Geological Survey (USGS) to produce population estimates using these data.

Methods

Data Collection

Mark-recapture surveys were conducted at 19 sites between 2004 and 2010. Surveys occurred three to four times per year during the second week in July, usually on consecutive days, but occasionally two surveys were conducted on a single day. Dipnetting was the sole sampling method used. Individual frogs measuring greater than 45-mm snout-vent length received Biomark™ 12-mm passive integrated transponder (PIT) tags. Sampling was approved annually by the Nevada Department of Wildlife.

USGS Database Review Process

The NNHP provided scans (.pdf format) of original data sheets along with a Microsoft© Access database. The original database consisted of one table containing all survey and capture data for surveys conducted from 2004 to 2010.

We reviewed and restructured the database with the intention of increasing accessibility for future mark-recapture analyses. We divided the original data table into survey and capture tables, and created reports with which to review the data. The new database is structured such that data entry and retrieval may be less prone to errors by more strictly defining the relationship between surveys and capture events, and by creating data entry forms.

All original data sheets and database reports were reconciled, and the restructured database encompasses all resulting corrections. Data definitions for the restructured database are provided in appendix A.

Analysis

We selected the Farrington, Jamie's, Pasture A North, and Warner's sites for our analysis because they provided both the largest populations of frogs and the most consistently collected data over the course of the study. In our analysis, the Jamie's and Pasture A North sites are treated as one site (hereafter "Pasture") because they are immediately adjacent to one another and are located along the same waterway. The Farrington and Warner's sites are isolated from each other and from the Pasture complex (fig. 2).

We used a Huggins Closed Captures Robust Design method in the program MARK (v 6.0; White and Burnham, 1999) to analyze the data. This model estimates annual survival (S), the probability that a member of the population is unavailable for capture (a temporary emigrant, γ''), the probability that an emigrant the previous year remains unavailable for capture in the current year (γ'), capture probability (p), and recapture probability (c). Population size (N) is not estimated, but can be derived from the model.

For notational purposes in this report, we use 'id' to represent the identity design matrix. For example, S(id) uses the identity matrix to estimate S parameters, which means that S is estimated independently for each year except the first. Survival cannot be estimated for the first year. We use '.' to indicate that no covariates are used to estimate a parameter, and thus that the parameter will be a single estimated value. In some cases, a parameter is set to be equal to another (for example, $\gamma''=\gamma'(.)$) or to another plus an offset (for example, p(id)=c+1). Using an offset allows p and c to differ by a set amount, but to vary from survey session to survey session in the same manner. We fit the following models:

1. $\{S(id)\gamma''=\gamma'(.)p(id)=c+1\}$ Random temporary emigration and recapture probability offset.
2. $\{S(id)\gamma''(.)\gamma'(.)p(id)=c+1\}$ Recapture probability offset of p.
3. $\{S(id)\gamma''=\gamma'(.)p(id)=c\}$ Random temporary emigration.
4. $\{S(id)\gamma''=\gamma'(.)p(year)=c+1\}$ Random temporary emigration, capture probability for each year but not each session, recapture probability offset of p.

All these models estimate S each year and allow N to be derived for each year. They only differ in the manner in which temporary emigration and capture probabilities are modeled. We chose the best model for each group based on AIC_c (Akaike's Information Criteria for small sample size) and on the success of the model at estimating parameters.

2

Results

Farrington

None of the models gave meaningful estimates of temporary emigration parameters, and there was little separation in AIC_c among models (table 1). We chose the random temporary emigration model for reporting due to its relative simplicity (fig. 3, table 2). Modeling recapture probability as an offset of p had very weak support and was retained. Modeling session to session, rather than year to year, variation in p=c+1 was strongly supported. Population size showed an overall increase, but the lowest estimate was in the 5th of 7 years (fig. 4, table 3).

Pasture

All models gave survival estimates for the final year that were near 1, which is unrealistically high (table 2, fig. 3). This was the only group of ponds that allowed reasonable estimates of temporary emigration, and it was very low with $\gamma''=\gamma'= 0.07$ (SE=0.1036) in the best model (appendix B). Random temporary emigration was only weakly supported, but the model with both γ'' and γ' did not produce meaningful estimates of γ'. Population size showed a generally-increasing trend (fig. 4, table 3), but the final year's estimate is somewhat suspect because of the problem with estimating S for that year.

Warner's

Estimates for γ'' were by far the highest for this site compared to the other sites ($\gamma''=0.56$, SE = 0.1702; $\gamma' = 0.95$, SE = 0.0863). There was support for separate estimates for γ'' and γ', but random temporary emigration could not be ruled out based on these data. Modeling recapture probability as an offset of p had moderate support, and modeling p=c for each session was strongly supported over a model that only estimated p=c+1 for each year. Population size decreased the first few years, but has since increased (fig. 4, table 3) and was at its all-time high in the last year reported (2010).

Estimates of model parameters (betas) for all sites are shown in appendix C.

Discussion

Other than Warner's, the models had problems with estimating temporary emigration. These problems may be due to a very low rate of temporary emigration at Farrington and Pasture. Low temporary emigration is suggested by the distance between the pond clusters and other suitable habitat, and by the models themselves, which gave imprecise but always low estimates. Conversely, Warner's appears to have a high rate of temporary emigration at 0.56, with emigrants almost always continuing their absence in subsequent years ($\gamma'= 0.95$).

Another difficulty encountered in the analysis was the lack of any explanatory variables for capture and recapture probability. Sex ratios appeared to be appropriately distributed, but we did not include sex in our analysis because of the high number of frogs identified as "unknown" (fig. 5, table 4). Air temperature was sometimes, but not always, recorded, as were habitat and other environmental variables. Estimating p=c+1 separately for each session was always strongly supported, suggesting that the conditions that affect capture probability were highly variable even within years (appendix B). Models would likely improve if some of the variation in capture probability could be explained by covariates. This might negate the need to do separate estimates for each sampling session.

We attempted to use a closed captures model that estimated all of the same parameters reported in this report, plus population size, so that we could attempt to model population size as a function of year, but these models had problems with many of the parameter estimates and often had singular estimates of population size. The Huggins models that we ultimately used performed better than the other models, but did not allow us to test hypotheses about trends in N within the model framework. The derived estimates of N can be used to gain a general understanding of trends in abundance. None of the three groups showed evidence of decline over the period of study.

Summary

The Toiyabe subpopulation of the Columbia spotted frog (*Rana luteiventris*) is located in central Nevada and is part of the Great Basin Distinct Population Segment (DPS). Columbia spotted frogs are of special concern as range-wide population declines have been documented, and the species is a candidate for listing under the Endangered Species Act. Multiple State and Federal agencies have cooperatively monitored this population over the last 7 years, and will continue to do so in the near future. We restructured the database and estimated population parameters using a Huggins Closed Captures Robust Design Model. Derived estimates of population size did not show evidence of decline over the study years.

Acknowledgments

We thank Jennifer Newmark and Kristin Szabo of the Nevada Natural Heritage Program; Jon Sjoberg, Teri Slatauski, and Brad Bauman of the Nevada Department of Wildlife; Jim Harvey and Steve Williams of the U.S. Forest Service; and Bob Williams and Selena Werdon of the U.S. Fish and Wildlife Service. This is product 434 of the Amphibian Research and Monitoring Initiative.

References Cited

Funk, W.C., Pearl, C.A., Draheim, H.M., Adams, M.J., Mullis, T.D., and Haig, S.M., 2008, Rangewide phylogenetic analysis of the spotted frog complex (*Rana luteiventris* and *Rana pretiosa*) in northwestern North America: Molecular Phylogenetics and Evolution, v. 49, p. 198–210.

Nevada Department of Wildlife, 2003, Conservation agreement and strategy for the Columbia spotted frog (*Rana luteiventris*)—Great Basin Population Nevada—Toiyabe subpopulation: Reno, Nevada, Nevada Department of Wildlife Interagency document, 43 p.

Nevada Department of Wildlife, 2004, Toiyabe spotted frog Great Basin subpopulation long-term monitoring plan: Las Vegas, Nevada Department of Wildlife, 25 p.

U.S. Fish and Wildlife Service, 2011, Species assessment and listing priority assignment form, Columbia spotted frog (*Rana luteiventris*), Great Basin Distinct Population Segment, Pacific Southwest Region, Sacramento, California, April 15, 2011, 44 p., accessed December 31, 2012, at http://ecos.fws.gov/speciesProfile/profile/speciesProfile.action?spcode=D027.

White, G.C., and Burnham, K. P., 1999, Program MARK—Survival estimation from populations of marked animals: Bird Study 46 supplement, p. 120–138.

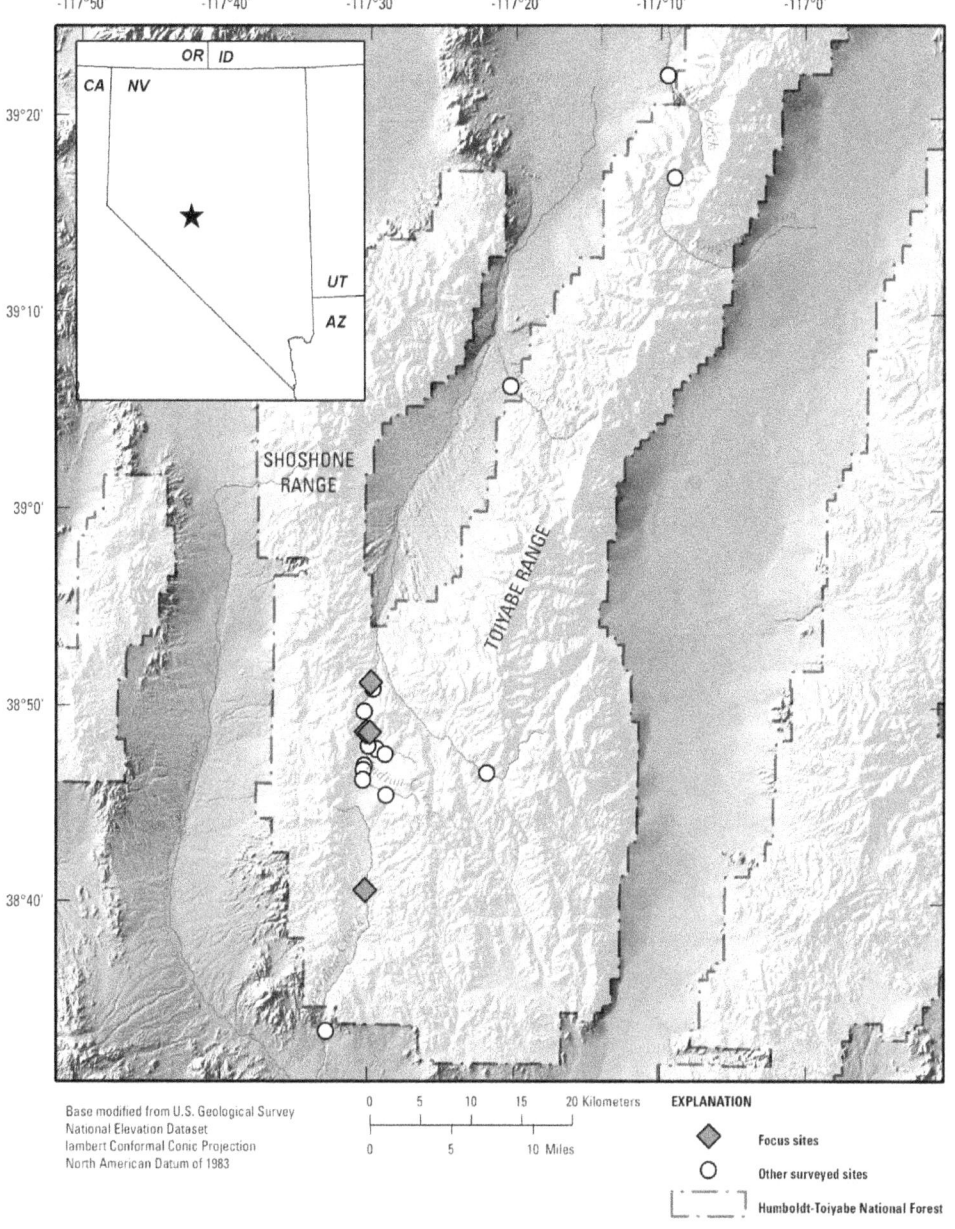

Figure 1. Map showing locations surveyed for Columbia spotted frogs (*Rana luteiventris*) in the Humboldt-Toiyabe National Forest, Nevada, 2004–10.

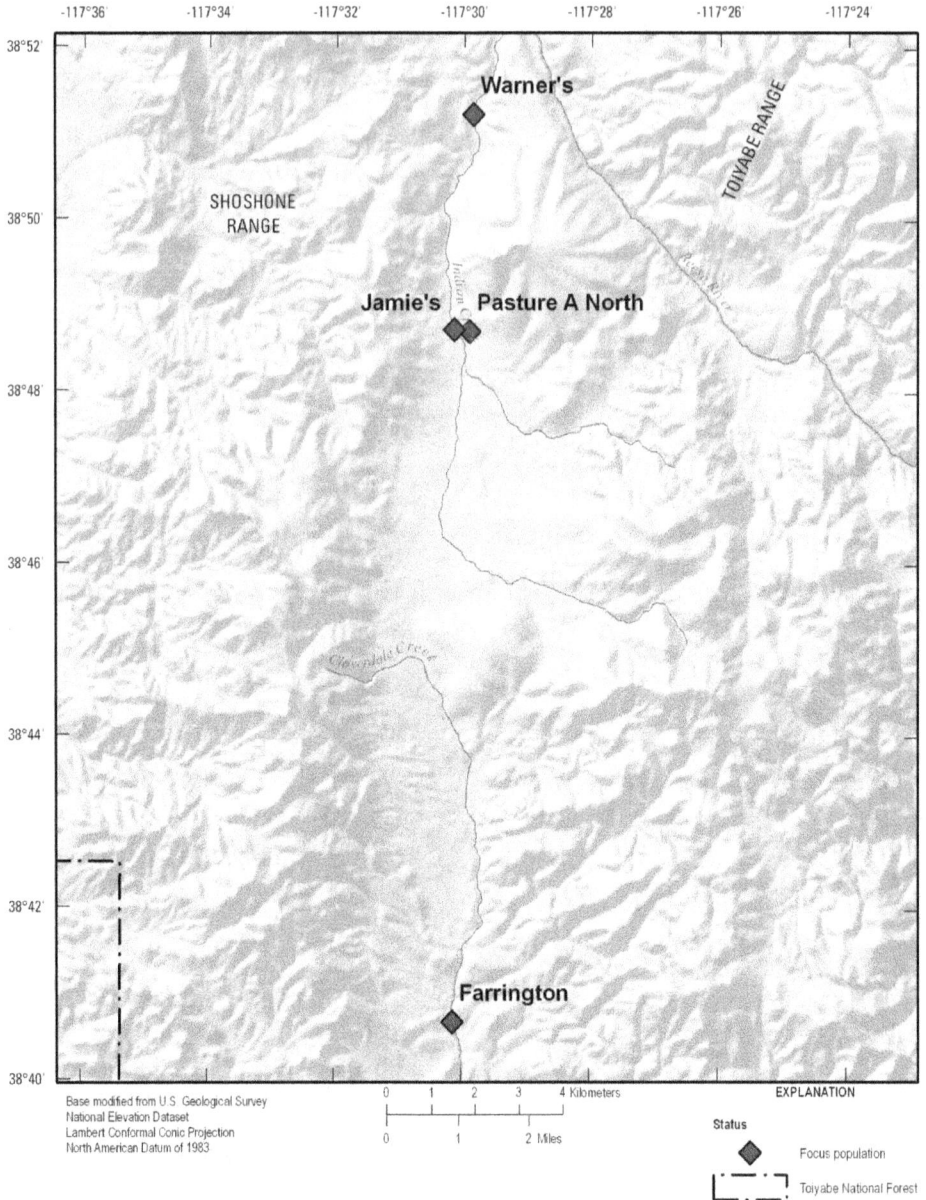

Figure 2. Map showing Warner's, Jamie's, Pasture A North, and Farrington survey locations in the Humboldt-Toiyabe National Forest, Nevada, 2004–10.

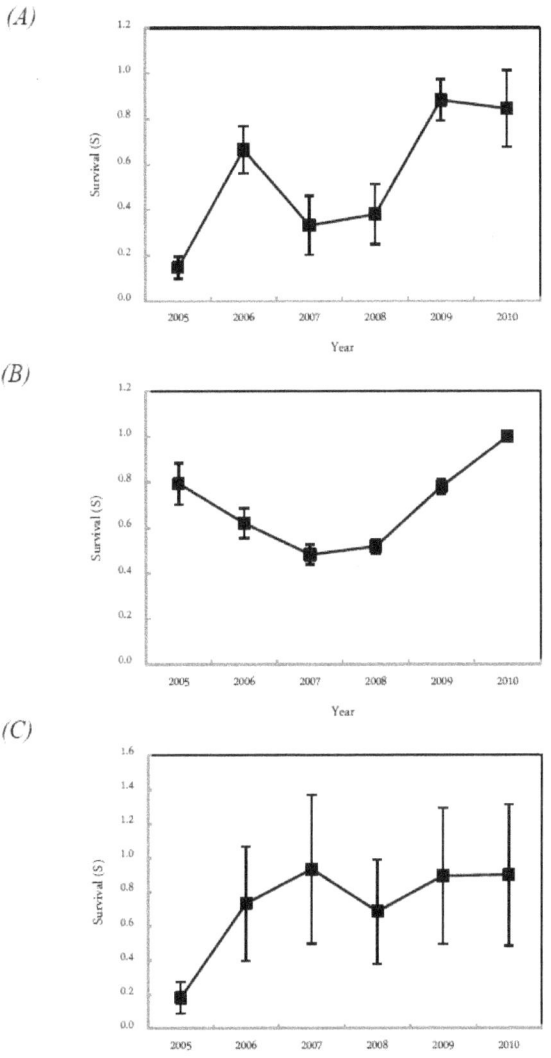

Figure 3. Graphs showing survival estimates (S) for each survey year for (A) Farrington, (B) Pasture, and (C) Warner's populations. Error bars represent standard error.

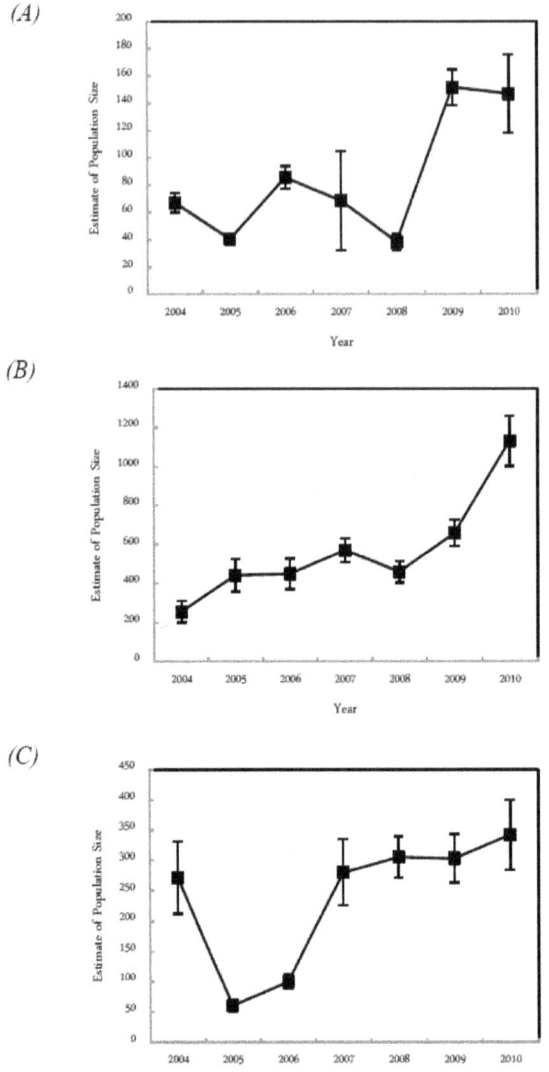

Figure 4. Graphs showing estimates of population size (N-hat) for each survey year for (A) Farrington, (B) Pasture, and (C) Warner's populations. Error bars represent standard error.

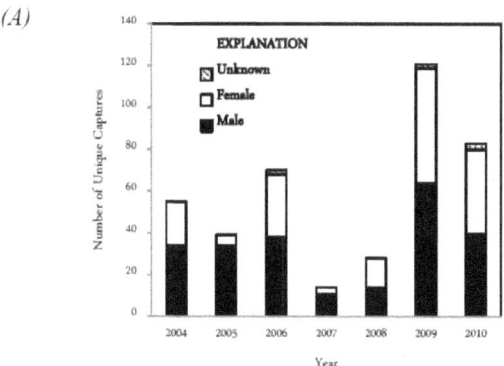

(A)

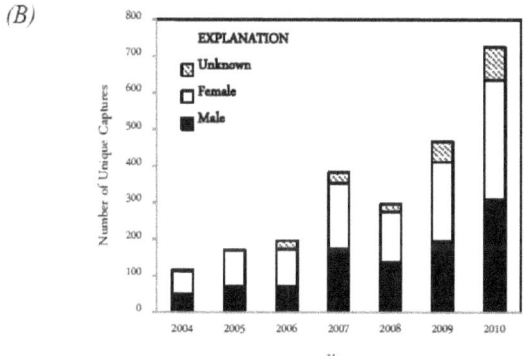

(B)

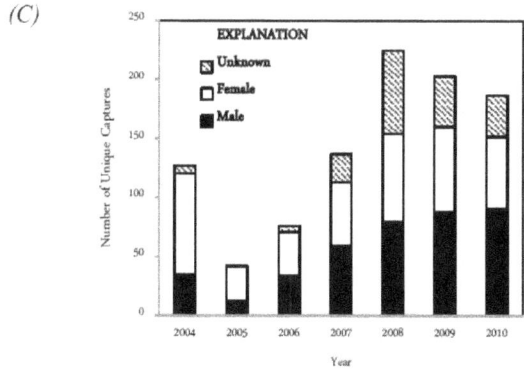

(C)

Figure 5. Graphs showing number of unique captures by sex within survey year for (A) Farrington, (B) Pasture, and (C) Warner's populations.

Table 1. Model ranks and selection statistics for models estimating population parameters for Columbia spotted frogs (*Rana luteiventris*) at three survey sites in central Nevada.

[Model: Models used in analysis. AIC_c : Akaike's Information Criteria for small sample size. ΔAIC_c: The difference between the AICc of the best model and a subsequent model. AICc Weight: The relative support for a particular model. Model Likelihood: The likelihood statistic. No. Parameters: The number of estimated parameters included in the model. Deviance: Residual deviance]

Model	AIC_c	ΔAIC_c	AIC_c weight	Model likelihood	Number of parameters	Deviance
			Farrington			
$\{S(id)\gamma''=\gamma'(.)p(id)=c+1\}$	2,248.625	0.00	0.37540	1.0000	30	2,332.703
$\{S(id)\gamma''(.)\gamma'(.)p(id)=c+1\}$	2,248.625	0.00	0.37540	1.0000	30	2,332.703
$\{S(id)\gamma''=\gamma'(.)p(id)=c\}$	2,249.444	0.82	0.24920	0.6638	30	2,333.522
$\{S(id)\gamma''=\gamma'(.)p(year)=c+1\}$	2,296.802	48.18	0.00000	0.0000	14	2,415.139
			Pasture			
$\{S(id)\gamma''=\gamma'(.)p(id)=c+1\}$	11,792.508	0.00	0.72961	1.0000	28	20,206.211
$\{S(id)\gamma''(.)\gamma'(.)p(id)=c+1\}$	11,794.498	1.99	0.26982	0.3698	29	20,206.169
$\{S(id)\gamma''(.)\gamma'(.)p(id)=c\}$	11,806.840	14.33	0.00056	0.0008	29	20,218.511
$\{S(id)\gamma''=\gamma'(.)p(year)=c+1\}$	11,863.087	70.58	0.00000	0.0000	14	20,305.126
			Warner's			
$\{S(id)\gamma''(.)\gamma'(.)p(id)=c+1\}$	5,792.997	0.00	0.88086	1.0000	36	6,369.730
$\{S(id)\gamma''=\gamma'(.)p(id)=c+1\}$	5,797.024	4.03	0.11761	0.1335	35	6,375.846
$\{S(id)\gamma''=\gamma'(.)p(id)=c\}$	5,805.701	12.70	0.00153	0.0017	34	6,386.611
$\{S(id)\gamma''=\gamma'(.)p(year)=c+1\}$	5,856.940	63.94	0.0000	0.0000	15	6,477.017

Table 2. Survival estimates (S) for Farrington, Pasture, and Warner's populations from 2005 to 2010.

[Standard error values are denoted in parentheses]

Year	Farrington	Pasture	Warner's
2005	0.1 (0.05)	0.8 (0.09)	0.2 (0.09)
2006	0.7 (0.10)	0.6 (0.07)	0.7 (0.34)
2007	0.3 (0.13)	0.5 (0.04)	0.9 (0.44)
2008	0.4 (0.13)	0.5 (0.03)	0.7 (0.31)
2009	0.9 (0.09)	0.8 (0.03)	0.9 (0.40)
2010	0.8 (0.17)	1.0 (0.00)	0.9 (0.41)

Table 3. Population estimates (N-hat) for Farrington, Pasture, and Warner's populations from 2004 to 2010.

[Standard error values are denoted in parentheses]

Year	Farrington	Pasture	Warner's
2004	67.3 (7.15)	256.5 (53.95)	271.2 (59.42)
2005	40.7 (1.66)	442.7 (83.99)	60.4 (9.71)
2006	85.8 (8.20)	450.0 (79.73)	99.5 (11.42)
2007	68.6 (36.15)	571.7 (62.41)	279.6 (54.44)
2008	38.6 (6.03)	460.0 (54.94)	304.9 (33.89)
2009	151.8 (13.18)	659.8 (67.47)	302.6 (39.67)
2010	147.1 (28.57)	1,129.9 (127.24)	341.7 (58.06)

Table 4. Number of unique captures, differentiated by sex, for Farrington, Pasture, and Warner's populations from 2004 to 2010.

Year	Male	Female	Unknown
Farrington			
2004	34	21	0
2005	34	5	0
2006	38	30	2
2007	11	3	0
2008	14	14	0
2009	64	55	2
2010	40	40	3
Pasture			
2004	51	62	3
2005	70	98	2
2006	70	103	22
2007	175	178	30
2008	138	138	20
2009	196	216	56
2010	310	326	89
Warner's			
2004	35	86	6
2005	12	30	0
2006	34	37	5
2007	59	54	24
2008	80	74	71
2009	88	72	43
2010	91	61	35

Appendix A. Database Field Descriptions.

Data table	Field name	Data type	Description
Surveys	SurveyID	AutoNumber	Unique identifier assigned to each survey record
Surveys	Site_Org	Text	Site name originally recorded on data sheet
Surveys	Site_Correct	Text	Corrected/standardized site name
Surveys	Year	Text	Year in which survey took place
Surveys	SurveyDate	Date/Time	Date on which survey took place (mm/dd/yyyy format)
Surveys	Pass_Time_Start	Date/Time	Time at which survey started (24-hour format)
Surveys	Pass_Time_End	Date/Time	Time at which survey ended (24-hour format)
Surveys	SurveyCompleted	Text	Indicates whether or not the survey was completed (yes/no)
Surveys	Pass_Code	Text	Pass/visit number for this survey (for example, 1, 2; or, when there are multiple crews conducting same pass at the same site, the pass number plus a modifier, for example, 1a, 1b, 1c)
Surveys	Pass_Number	Number	Number assigned to the survey pass in its entirety
Surveys	SurveyCrew	Text	Names of crew members conducting the survey
Surveys	StartUTME	Number	UTM easting coordinate of survey starting point
Surveys	StartUTMN	Number	UTM northing coordinate of survey starting point
Surveys	EndUTME	Number	UTM easting coordinate of survey ending point
Surveys	EndUTMN	Number	UTM northing coordinate of survey ending point
Surveys	Datum	Text	Datum in which coordinates were taken
Surveys	SiteType	Text	Describes the type of site being surveyed
Surveys	SurveyType	Text	Indicates what type of survey was conducted (egg mass, presence/absence, pond, or mark/recapture).
Surveys	Sky	Text	Cloud conditions during the survey; originally included in a Svy_Weather field
Surveys	Wind	Text	Wind conditions during the survey; originally included in a Svy_Weather field
Surveys	Precip	Text	Precipitation conditions during the survey; originally included in a Svy_Weather field
Surveys	StartAirTemp	Number	Air temperature at the start of the survey
Surveys	StartWaterTemp	Number	Water temperature at the start of the survey
Surveys	EndAirTemp	Number	Air temperature at the end of the survey
Surveys	EndWaterTemp	Number	Water temperature at the end of the survey
Surveys	TempScale	Text	Scale in which temperatures were taken (Celsius or Fahrenheit).
Surveys	Breeding	Text	Indicates whether or not breeding (that is, life stages that indicate breeding occurred at this site) was detected during the entire survey.

Appendix A. Database Field Descriptions–Continued.

Data table	Field name	Data type	Description
Surveys	AvailHabitat	Text	An evaluation of suitable frog habitat available at the survey site. Values are: low (moist habitat mostly restricted to main water course, ephemeral ponds dry or drying), mod (most moist habitat and ephemeral ponds inundated with water but beginning to dry out), and high (moist habitats well inundated with water, ephemeral ponds to not appear in danger of drying out during breeding season).
Surveys	WaterClarity	Text	Indicates the clarity of the majority of the water at the survey site. Values are clear, murky, and cloudy.
Surveys	WaterColor	Text	Indicates the color of most of the water at the survey site. Values are clear, brown, green, and milky.
Surveys	Grazing	Text	Indicates whether or not evidence of grazing was observed during the survey.
Surveys	Trampling	Text	Indicates whether or not trampling from grazing animals had occurred at the survey site.
Surveys	SurveyNotes	Memo	Any notes relevant to this particular survey
Surveys	USGS_comment	Text	Notes from USGS database review
Captures	CaptureID	AutoNumber	Unique identifier assigned to this particular capture record
Captures	Site_Correct	Text	Corrected/standardized site name
Captures	SurveyDate	Date/Time	Date on which survey took place (mm/dd/yyyy format)
Captures	Pass_Code	Text	Pass/visit number for this survey (for example, 1, 2; or, when there are multiple crews conducting same pass at the same site, the pass number plus a modifier, for example, 1a, 1b, 1c)
Captures	Pass_Number	Number	Number assigned to the survey pass in its entirety
Captures	IndivUTME	Number	UTM easting coordinate at which this frog was captured
Captures	IndivUTMN	Number	UTM northing coordinate at which this frog was captured
Captures	Datum	Text	Datum in which the capture coordinates were taken
Captures	Substrate	Text	Substrate on which frog was captured
Captures	MarkRecap	Text	Indication of whether or not this frog has been captured before
Captures	Tag_old	Text	PIT tag number provided in the original/uncorrected database (this field should not be populated when new (post-2010) records are added).
Captures	Tag	Text	QA'd PIT tag number (USGS QA through 2010)
Captures	IndivTime	Date/Time	Time at which frog was captured (24-hour format)
Captures	SNVL_MM	Number	Snout-vent length, in millimeters, of frog

Appendix A. Database Field Descriptions–Continued.

Data table	Field name	Data type	Description
Captures	Sex	Text	Sex of frog (male, female, or unknown).
Captures	IndivNotes	Text	Notes relevant to this particular capture record
Captures	USGS_caps_comment	Text	Notes from USGS database review
Captures	QA	Yes/No	Indicates whether or not this record has been QA'd after entry into database
Captures	OldID	Number	Old identifier that may be used to connect corrected database with uncorrected database. This field should not be populated when new (post-2010) records are added.
Captures	Delete	Yes/No	Indicates whether or not this record should be deleted from the database
Captures	NNHP_COMMENT	Text	These data were generated post-field and were not QA'd by USGS
Captures	Age	Text	These data were generated post-field and were not QA'd by USGS
Captures	Tads	Yes/No	These data were generated post-field and were not QA'd by USGS
Captures	InBiotics	Yes/No	These data were generated post-field and were not QA'd by USGS
Captures	NNHP_MAP_COMMENT	Text	These data were generated post-field and were not QA'd by USGS
Captures	CORRECTED_NAD83_X	Number	These data were generated post-field and were not QA'd by USGS
Captures	CORRECTED_NAD83_Y	Number	These data were generated post-field and were not QA'd by USGS
Captures	IndivUTME(27)	Number	These data were generated post-field and were not QA'd by USGS
Captures	IndivUTMN(27)	Number	These data were generated post-field and were not QA'd by USGS
Captures	IndivUTME(83)	Number	These data were generated post-field and were not QA'd by USGS
Captures	IndivUTMN(83)	Number	These data were generated post-field and were not QA'd by USGS
Captures	SNVL_NOTGOOD	Yes/No	These data were generated post-field and were not QA'd by USGS
Antennae	AntID	AutoNumber	Unique identifier assigned to this particular antenna record
Antennae	Site_ORG	Text	Site at which antenna was deployed
Antennae	Site_CORRECT	Text	Corrected/standardized site name
Antennae	SiteID	Text	Identifier assigned to antenna deployment location
Antennae	AntennaNumber	Text	Unique identifier for this antenna
Antennae	DetectDate	Date/Time	Date (mm/dd/yy format) on which this detection was made
Antennae	DetectTime	Date/Time	Time (24-hour format) at which this detection was made
Antennae	AntCode	Text	Code, if any, provided by antenna

Appendix A. Database Field Descriptions–Continued.

Data table	Field name	Data type	Description
Antennae	Tag	Text	PIT tag number of detected frog
Antennae	AntUTME	Number	Easting coordinate of antenna, in NAD83
Antennae	AntUTMN	AntUTMN	Northing coordinate of antenna, in NAD83
Antennae	AntNotes	Text	Any notes relevant to this particular record.
JuvenilesAndStragglers	JSID	AutoNumber	Unique identifier assigned to this particular capture record
JuvenilesAndStragglers	OldID	Number	Old identifier that may be used to connect corrected database with un-QA'd database. This field should not be populated when new (post-2010) records are added.
JuvenilesAndStragglers	SITE_CORRECT	Text	Corrected/standardized site name
JuvenilesAndStragglers	SurveyDate	Date/Time	Date on which survey took place (mm/dd/yyyy format)
JuvenilesAndStragglers	Pass_Code	Text	Pass/visit number for this survey (for example, 1, 2; or, when there are multiple crews conducting same pass at the same site, the pass number plus a modifier, for example, 1a, 1b, 1c)
JuvenilesAndStragglers	Pass_Number	Number	Number assigned to the survey pass in its entirety
JuvenilesAndStragglers	IndivUTME	Number	UTM easting coordinate at which this frog was captured
JuvenilesAndStragglers	IndivUTMN	Number	UTM northing coordinate at which this frog was captured
JuvenilesAndStragglers	Datum	Text	Datum in which the capture coordinates were taken
JuvenilesAndStragglers	Substrate	Text	Substrate on which frog was captured (water, mud, algae, bare ground, sedge, rush, sand, gravel, cobble, boulder, emergent vegetation, grass, or other)
JuvenilesAndStragglers	MarkRecap	Text	Indication of whether or not this frog has been captured before
JuvenilesAndStragglers	IndivMark	Text	Indication or note of individual mark (Note: all frogs with readable PIT tags should be entered in the Captures table)
JuvenilesAndStragglers	IndivTime	Date/Time	Time at which frog was captured (24-hour format)
JuvenilesAndStragglers	SNVL_MM	Number	Snout-vent length, in millimeters of frog
JuvenilesAndStragglers	Sex	Text	Sex of frog (male, female, juvenile, or unknown)
JuvenilesAndStragglers	IndivNotes	Text	Comments made by surveyor as noted on the survey form.
JuvenilesAndStragglers	USGS_caps_comment	Text	Notes from USGS database review
JuvenilesAndStragglers	SNVL_NOTGOOD	Yes/No	These data were generated post-field and were not QA'd by USGS
JuvenilesAndStragglers	NNHP_COMMENT	Text	These data were generated post-field and were not QA'd by USGS
JuvenilesAndStragglers	NNHP_MAP_COMMENT	Text	These data were generated post-field and were not QA'd by USGS

Appendix A. Database Field Descriptions–Continued.

Data table	Field name	Data type	Description
JuvenilesAndStragglers	AGE	Text	These data were generated post-field and were not QA'd by USGS
JuvenilesAndStragglers	INBIOTICS	Yes/No	These data were generated post-field and were not QA'd by USGS
JuvenilesAndStragglers	TADS_PRESENT	Yes/No	These data were generated post-field and were not QA'd by USGS
JuvenilesAndStragglers	IndivUTME(27)	Number	These data were generated post-field and were not QA'd by USGS
JuvenilesAndStragglers	IndivUTMN(27)	Number	These data were generated post-field and were not QA'd by USGS
JuvenilesAndStragglers	IndivUTME(83)	Number	These data were generated post-field and were not QA'd by USGS
JuvenilesAndStragglers	IndivUTMN(83)	Number	These data were generated post-field and were not QA'd by USGS
JuvenilesAndStragglers	CORRECTED_NAD83_X	Number	These data were generated post-field and were not QA'd by USGS
JuvenilesAndStragglers	CORRECTED_NAD83_Y	Number	These data were generated post-field and were not QA'd by USGS

Appendix B. Real Parameter Estimates for the Random Temporary Emigration Model at Three Survey Sites.

[Parameter: The parameter estimated. Estimate: The estimate of this parameter. Standard Error: Standard error of the parameter estimate. 95-percent confidence level (lower) and 95-percent confidence level (upper) are the lower and upper confidence limits of the parameter estimates]

Population	Parameter	Estimate	Standard Error	95 % CI (lower)	95 % CI (upper)
Farrington	1:S	0.1481162	0.0484372	0.0757280	0.2695223
Farrington	2:S	0.6643109	0.1036068	0.4432329	0.8310633
Farrington	3:S	0.3318729	0.1285315	0.1375400	0.6074059
Farrington	4:S	0.3797080	0.1313377	0.1702671	0.6461503
Farrington	5:S	0.8813228	0.0907867	0.5753557	0.9760208
Farrington	6:S	0.8438631	0.1679646	0.3076049	0.9850187
Farrington	7:Gamma"	0.0000001	0.0000679	0.0000000	1.0000000
Farrington	8:Gamma"	0.0000001	0.0000679	0.0000000	1.0000000
Farrington	9:Gamma"	0.0000001	0.0000679	0.0000000	1.0000000
Farrington	10:Gamma"	0.0000001	0.0000679	0.0000000	1.0000000
Farrington	11:Gamma"	0.0000001	0.0000679	0.0000000	1.0000000
Farrington	12:Gamma"	0.0000001	0.0000679	0.0000000	1.0000000
Farrington	13:Gamma'	0.0000001	0.0000679	0.0000000	1.0000000
Farrington	14:Gamma'	0.0000001	0.0000679	0.0000000	1.0000000
Farrington	15:Gamma'	0.0000001	0.0000679	0.0000000	1.0000000
Farrington	16:Gamma'	0.0000001	0.0000679	0.0000000	1.0000000
Farrington	17:Gamma'	0.0000001	0.0000679	0.0000000	1.0000000
Farrington	18:p Session 1	0.6243012	0.0888439	0.4416237	0.7773458
Farrington	19:p Session 1	0.3352674	0.0870530	0.1899930	0.5202745

18

Appendix B. Real Parameter Estimates for the Random Temporary Emigration Model at Three Survey Sites—Continued.

Population	Parameter	Estimate	Standard Error	95 % CI (lower)	95 % CI (upper)
Farrington	20:p Session 1	0.2693874	0.0833822	0.1384659	0.4582536
Farrington	21:p Session 2	0.7659508	0.0725391	0.5968844	0.8785396
Farrington	22:p Session 2	0.1683745	0.0648435	0.0755195	0.3341350
Farrington	23:p Session 2	0.7018002	0.0975862	0.4854871	0.8544375
Farrington	24:p Session 2	0.2931777	0.0917481	0.1483268	0.4969461
Farrington	25:p Session 3	0.3183346	0.0583282	0.2161446	0.4416189
Farrington	26:p Session 3	0.2664166	0.0611075	0.1644189	0.4013002
Farrington	27:p Session 3	0.4165133	0.0852748	0.2640873	0.5867692
Farrington	28:p Session 3	0.3699742	0.0896557	0.2164948	0.5551636
Farrington	29:p Session 4	0.1019106	0.0575391	0.0320349	0.2800980
Farrington	30:p Session 4	0.1136237	0.0620063	0.0369349	0.2999505
Farrington	31:p Session 5	0.3082242	0.0830307	0.1719774	0.4887039
Farrington	32:p Session 5	0.2665139	0.0811798	0.1386770	0.4505517
Farrington	33:p Session 5	0.4589758	0.1088250	0.2643585	0.6669681
Farrington	34:p Session 6	0.3974703	0.0508212	0.3032340	0.4999778
Farrington	35:p Session 6	0.3281674	0.0609489	0.2212635	0.4564475
Farrington	36:p Session 6	0.2552881	0.0595920	0.1564387	0.3878778
Farrington	37:p Session 6	0.3262262	0.0730958	0.2014743	0.4816328
Farrington	38:p Session 7	0.1836020	0.0478721	0.1073490	0.2960554
Farrington	39:p Session 7	0.3293946	0.0817214	0.1921590	0.5035483
Farrington	40:p Session 7	0.2043678	0.0639352	0.1062253	0.3569698
Farrington	41:c Session 1	0.3934773	0.0672763	0.2718527	0.5299157
Farrington	42:c Session 1	0.3216946	0.0625100	0.2129092	0.4540023

Appendix B. Real Parameter Estimates for the Random Temporary Emigration Model at Three Survey Sites–Continued.

Population	Parameter	Estimate	Standard Error	95 % CI (lower)	95 % CI (upper)
Farrington	43:c Session 2	0.2066147	0.0654468	0.1064070	0.3628704
Farrington	44:c Session 2	0.7516856	0.0713048	0.5887676	0.8648736
Farrington	45:c Session 2	0.3479046	0.0757194	0.2171361	0.5064771
Farrington	46:c Session 3	0.3183983	0.0602675	0.2132506	0.4460006
Farrington	47:c Session 3	0.4786716	0.0620680	0.3605759	0.5992004
Farrington	48:c Session 3	0.4303093	0.0598436	0.3188507	0.5493091
Farrington	49:c Session 4	0.1415456	0.0776679	0.0449884	0.3659327
Farrington	50:c Session 5	0.3185064	0.0887666	0.1733334	0.5102227
Farrington	51:c Session 5	0.5218040	0.0975280	0.3365280	0.7012690
Farrington	52:c Session 6	0.3858602	0.0480615	0.2968663	0.4831988
Farrington	53:c Session 6	0.3060042	0.0414930	0.2311515	0.3927152
Farrington	54:c Session 6	0.3837726	0.0437261	0.3023862	0.4722358
Farrington	55:c Session 7	0.3871788	0.0644846	0.2705436	0.5183651
Farrington	56:c Session 7	0.2483414	0.0481931	0.1661029	0.3540112
Pasture	1:S	0.7934131	0.0906777	0.5649584	0.9190817
Pasture	2:S	0.6195360	0.0656543	0.4854158	0.7375961
Pasture	3:S	0.4825586	0.0430749	0.3994127	0.5666815
Pasture	4:S	0.5181298	0.0299052	0.4595351	0.5762300
Pasture	5:S	0.7794672	0.0328805	0.7084064	0.8371906
Pasture	6:S	0.9999933	0.0009360	0.0000000	1.0000000
Pasture	7:Gamma"	0.0703721	0.1036381	0.0033816	0.6280928
Pasture	8:Gamma"	0.0703721	0.1036381	0.0033816	0.6280928
Pasture	9:Gamma"	0.0703721	0.1036381	0.0033816	0.6280928

Appendix B. Real Parameter Estimates for the Random Temporary Emigration Model at Three Survey Sites–Continued.

Population	Parameter	Estimate	Standard Error	95 % CI (lower)	95 % CI (upper)
Pasture	10:Gamma"	0.0703721	0.1036381	0.0033816	0.6280928
Pasture	11:Gamma"	0.0703721	0.1036381	0.0033816	0.6280928
Pasture	12:Gamma"	0.0703721	0.1036381	0.0033816	0.6280928
Pasture	13:Gamma'	0.0703721	0.1036381	0.0033816	0.6280928
Pasture	14:Gamma'	0.0703721	0.1036381	0.0033816	0.6280928
Pasture	15:Gamma'	0.0703721	0.1036381	0.0033816	0.6280928
Pasture	16:Gamma'	0.0703721	0.1036381	0.0033816	0.6280928
Pasture	17:Gamma'	0.0703721	0.1036381	0.0033816	0.6280928
Pasture	18:p Session 1	0.0896773	0.0259649	0.0501645	0.1552265
Pasture	19:p Session 1	0.2276308	0.0567707	0.1353312	0.3568980
Pasture	20:p Session 1	0.2210129	0.0603081	0.1249528	0.3604975
Pasture	21:p Session 2	0.1572909	0.0330528	0.1027284	0.2332983
Pasture	22:p Session 2	0.2208128	0.0489899	0.1395520	0.3311793
Pasture	23:p Session 2	0.0619426	0.0184537	0.0342217	0.1095711
Pasture	24:p Session 3	0.1960237	0.0377754	0.1322586	0.2805906
Pasture	25:p Session 3	0.1738992	0.0396490	0.1091754	0.2655555
Pasture	26:p Session 3	0.1467773	0.0375143	0.0872863	0.2363171
Pasture	27:p Session 4	0.3435361	0.0418298	0.2667605	0.4294660
Pasture	28:p Session 4	0.2856483	0.0520618	0.1951819	0.3973442
Pasture	29:p Session 4	0.2961199	0.0623097	0.1897288	0.4304749
Pasture	30:p Session 5	0.2695768	0.0376806	0.2023220	0.3493956
Pasture	31:p Session 5	0.3306650	0.0580922	0.2280019	0.4524615
Pasture	32:p Session 5	0.2707480	0.0592516	0.1709351	0.4006766

Appendix B. Real Parameter Estimates for the Random Temporary Emigration Model at Three Survey Sites—Continued.

Population	Parameter	Estimate	Standard Error	95 % CI (lower)	95 % CI (upper)
Pasture	33:p Session 6	0.3122192	0.0372324	0.2442350	0.3893774
Pasture	34:p Session 6	0.3368000	0.0564277	0.2363616	0.4545153
Pasture	35:p Session 6	0.3627017	0.0722392	0.2357360	0.5122191
Pasture	36:p Session 7	0.2859250	0.0340773	0.2240198	0.3570653
Pasture	37:p Session 7	0.2818106	0.0482435	0.1973890	0.3850181
Pasture	38:p Session 7	0.2977610	0.0612369	0.1927890	0.4294792
Pasture	39:c Session 1	0.3850003	0.0565250	0.2816511	0.4998827
Pasture	40:c Session 1	0.3760345	0.0520336	0.2806830	0.4820698
Pasture	41:c Session 2	0.3757618	0.0421415	0.2974007	0.4612164
Pasture	42:c Session 2	0.1230086	0.0213274	0.0869279	0.1712562
Pasture	43:c Session 3	0.3089822	0.0332075	0.2479230	0.3775306
Pasture	44:c Session 3	0.2676175	0.0289368	0.2148197	0.3279715
Pasture	45:c Session 4	0.4592768	0.0276669	0.4057383	0.5137721
Pasture	46:c Session 4	0.4719086	0.0259168	0.4215739	0.5228210
Pasture	47:c Session 5	0.5120428	0.0301457	0.4530639	0.5706882
Pasture	48:c Session 5	0.4409096	0.0278366	0.3872702	0.4959648
Pasture	49:c Session 6	0.5189340	0.0247375	0.4704224	0.5670912
Pasture	50:c Session 6	0.5472839	0.0242007	0.4995642	0.5941499
Pasture	51:c Session 7	0.4545908	0.0212338	0.4133833	0.4964298
Pasture	52:c Session 7	0.4738680	0.0185537	0.4377047	0.5103076
Warner's	1:S	0.1811069	0.0925544	0.0611086	0.4290606
Warner's	2:S	0.7322527	0.3353765	0.0873301	0.9873684
Warner's	3:S	0.9329104	0.4354087	1.67E-05	0.9999999

Appendix B. Real Parameter Estimates for the Random Temporary Emigration Model at Three Survey Sites–Continued.

Population	Parameter	Estimate	Standard Error	95 % CI (lower)	95 % CI (upper)
Warner's	4:S	0.6843547	0.3058341	0.1190841	0.9720461
Warner's	5:S	0.8926376	0.3991583	0.0023629	0.9999657
Warner's	6:S	0.8975479	0.4124239	0.0013311	0.9999826
Warner's	7:Gamma"	0.5659373	0.1701823	0.2511386	0.8352274
Warner's	8:Gamma"	0.5659373	0.1701823	0.2511386	0.8352274
Warner's	9:Gamma"	0.5659373	0.1701823	0.2511386	0.8352274
Warner's	10:Gamma"	0.5659373	0.1701823	0.2511386	0.8352274
Warner's	11:Gamma"	0.5659373	0.1701823	0.2511386	0.8352274
Warner's	12:Gamma"	0.5659373	0.1701823	0.2511386	0.8352274
Warner's	13:Gamma'	0.9506302	0.0862954	0.3438696	0.9985885
Warner's	14:Gamma'	0.9506302	0.0862954	0.3438696	0.9985885
Warner's	15:Gamma'	0.9506302	0.0862954	0.3438696	0.9985885
Warner's	16:Gamma'	0.9506302	0.0862954	0.3438696	0.9985885
Warner's	17:Gamma'	0.9506302	0.0862954	0.3438696	0.9985885
Warner's	18:p Session 1	0.1474773	0.0388247	0.086292	0.240621
Warner's	19:p Session 1	0.0828038	0.0261934	0.0439049	0.1507329
Warner's	20:p Session 1	0.1571457	0.0467498	0.0853781	0.2713428
Warner's	21:p Session 1	0.1931467	0.0592339	0.1020481	0.3352105
Warner's	22:p Session 2	0.2558797	0.068788	0.1448489	0.411104
Warner's	23:p Session 2	0.2916179	0.0795831	0.1621085	0.4669344
Warner's	24:p Session 2	0.2264889	0.0720971	0.1155924	0.3961245
Warner's	25:p Session 2	0.2518165	0.0806133	0.127019	0.4377453
Warner's	26:p Session 3	0.1229542	0.0358049	0.0681459	0.2118234

Appendix B. Real Parameter Estimates for the Random Temporary Emigration Model at Three Survey Sites—Continued.

Population	Parameter	Estimate	Standard Error	95 % CI (lower)	95 % CI (upper)
Warner's	27:p Session 3	0.4155048	0.0718093	0.284797	0.5592899
Warner's	28:p Session 3	0.2500315	0.0646108	0.1450721	0.3957745
Warner's	29:p Session 3	0.3847418	0.0927395	0.2248975	0.5740541
Warner's	30:p Session 4	0.1658622	0.0385766	0.1032386	0.2556436
Warner's	31:p Session 4	0.2201781	0.0544912	0.1316257	0.3446597
Warner's	32:p Session 4	0.122299	0.0372184	0.0659629	0.215641
Warner's	33:p Session 4	0.1067102	0.0343872	0.055627	0.1950166
Warner's	34:p Session 5	0.2809899	0.0405891	0.20861	0.3668419
Warner's	35:p Session 5	0.2462583	0.0490183	0.1629724	0.354101
Warner's	36:p Session 5	0.3103885	0.0675764	0.1951181	0.4552409
Warner's	37:p Session 5	0.2990562	0.0739632	0.1760465	0.4600288
Warner's	38:p Session 6	0.2381731	0.0395316	0.1694198	0.3239456
Warner's	39:p Session 6	0.2776269	0.0556345	0.1824277	0.3983029
Warner's	40:p Session 6	0.1803224	0.0463044	0.106387	0.2890218
Warner's	41:p Session 6	0.2701971	0.0676009	0.1590183	0.4202626
Warner's	42:p Session 7	0.2839083	0.054062	0.1905634	0.4003613
Warner's	43:p Session 7	0.2549642	0.0614408	0.1536492	0.3921325
Warner's	44:p Session 7	0.1515265	0.0437752	0.0839359	0.2582043
Warner's	45:c Session 1	0.1713358	0.0343525	0.1140101	0.2493726
Warner's	46:c Session 1	0.299231	0.0418186	0.2241153	0.3869665
Warner's	47:c Session 1	0.3541073	0.0441682	0.2729836	0.444596
Warner's	48:c Session 2	0.4852839	0.0832198	0.3291813	0.6443116
Warner's	49:c Session 2	0.4014119	0.0765434	0.2642566	0.5559619

Appendix B. Real Parameter Estimates for the Random Temporary Emigration Model at Three Survey Sites–Continued.

Population	Parameter	Estimate	Standard Error	95 % CI (lower)	95 % CI (upper)
Warner's	50:c Session 2	0.4352925	0.075799	0.2963634	0.5851853
Warner's	51:c Session 3	0.6194946	0.0655118	0.4856735	0.7373284
Warner's	52:c Session 3	0.4329595	0.058984	0.3228539	0.5501098
Warner's	53:c Session 3	0.588844	0.0583667	0.471699	0.6967148
Warner's	54:c Session 4	0.3927014	0.0458397	0.3073148	0.4851947
Warner's	55:c Session 4	0.2419205	0.0345531	0.1807226	0.3158523
Warner's	56:c Session 4	0.214816	0.0318476	0.1589295	0.2837252
Warner's	57:c Session 5	0.4280013	0.038782	0.3542295	0.5051193
Warner's	58:c Session 5	0.507588	0.0340896	0.4410333	0.5738749
Warner's	59:c Session 5	0.4942157	0.0340895	0.4278972	0.5607384
Warner's	60:c Session 6	0.4681419	0.0396601	0.3917867	0.5460187
Warner's	61:c Session 6	0.3350334	0.0331015	0.2735426	0.4026849
Warner's	62:c Session 6	0.4588521	0.0351357	0.3911913	0.5280649
Warner's	63:c Session 7	0.4393868	0.0405805	0.3620338	0.5198009
Warner's	64:c Session 7	0.2902809	0.0325882	0.2307545	0.3580163

25

Appendix C. Beta Estimates for the Random Temporary Emigration Model at Three Survey Sites.

[Parameter: Parameter estimated. Beta: Beta estimate generated for this parameter. Standard Error: Standard error of the parameter estimate. 95% CI-Lower and 95% CI-Upper are the lower and upper confidence limits of the beta estimates]

Population	Parameter	Beta	Standard Error	95% CI - Lower	95% CI - Upper
Farrington	1:S	-1.7494533	0.3838805	-2.5018590	-0.9970476
Farrington	2:S	0.6825649	0.4646004	-0.2280518	1.5931816
Farrington	3:S	-0.6997265	0.5796671	-1.8358741	0.4364211
Farrington	4:S	-0.4907877	0.5576264	-1.5837355	0.6021601
Farrington	5:S	2.0050166	0.8679999	0.3037367	3.7062965
Farrington	6:S	1.6872571	1.2747948	-0.8113408	4.1858549
Farrington	7:g	-16.6904470	1,203.6694000	-2,375.8826000	2,342.5017000
Farrington	8:p	0.5078451	0.3787857	-0.2345749	1.2502651
Farrington	9:p	-0.6844565	0.3906118	-1.4500557	0.0811426
Farrington	10:p	-0.9977330	0.4236519	-1.8280909	-0.1673752
Farrington	11:p	1.1855865	0.4046358	0.3925002	1.9786727
Farrington	12:p	-1.5971913	0.4630864	-2.5048407	-0.6895418
Farrington	13:p	0.8558848	0.4663024	-0.0580678	1.7698374
Farrington	14:p	-0.8800003	0.4427473	-1.7477850	-0.0122156
Farrington	15:p	-0.7614358	0.2687966	-1.2882772	-0.2345945
Farrington	16:p	-1.0128803	0.3126681	-1.6257098	-0.4000507
Farrington	17:p	-0.3371033	0.3508819	-1.0248320	0.3506253
Farrington	18:p	-0.5323274	0.3846345	-1.2862110	0.2215563
Farrington	19:p	-2.1761737	0.6286724	-3.4083716	-0.9439757
Farrington	20:p	-2.0542496	0.6156713	-3.2609654	-0.8475338
Farrington	21:p	-0.8084346	0.3894095	-1.5716772	-0.0451920
Farrington	22:p	-1.0123820	0.4152755	-1.8263220	-0.1984420

Appendix C. Beta Estimates for the Random Temporary Emigration Model at Three Survey Sites–Continued.

Population	Parameter	Beta	Standard Error	95% CI - Lower	95% CI - Upper
Farrington	23:p	-0.1644665	0.4382502	-1.0234370	0.6945040
Farrington	24:p	-0.4160169	0.2122082	-0.8319449	-0.0000888
Farrington	25:p	-0.7164855	0.2764452	-1.2583182	-0.1746528
Farrington	26:p	-1.0706048	0.3134507	-1.6849683	-0.4562414
Farrington	27:p	-0.7253036	0.3325519	-1.3771053	-0.0735019
Farrington	28:p	-1.4921319	0.3193770	-2.1181108	-0.8661531
Farrington	29:p	-0.7109244	0.3699580	-1.4360420	0.0141932
Farrington	30:p	-1.3592159	0.3932017	-2.1298912	-0.5885405
Farrington	31:c offset	0.2517379	0.2828872	-0.3027211	0.8061969
Pasture	1:S	1.3456226	0.5532205	0.2613103	2.4299349
Pasture	2:S	0.4875792	0.2785370	-0.0583534	1.0335117
Pasture	3:S	-0.0697941	0.1725095	-0.4079127	0.2683246
Pasture	4:S	0.0725508	0.1197783	-0.1622146	0.3073162
Pasture	5:S	1.2625643	0.1912792	0.8876571	1.6374715
Pasture	6:S	11.9071260	138.8263000	-260.1924300	284.0066900
Pasture	7:g	-2.5809872	1.5841993	-5.6860178	0.5240435
Pasture	8:p	-2.3175818	0.3180604	-2.9409803	-1.6941834
Pasture	9:p	-1.2217374	0.3229000	-1.8546213	-0.5888534
Pasture	10:p	-1.2597736	0.3502899	-1.9463417	-0.5732054
Pasture	11:p	-1.6785249	0.2493598	-2.1672701	-1.1897797
Pasture	12:p	-1.2609361	0.2847347	-1.8190160	-0.7028561
Pasture	13:p	-2.7176024	0.3175883	-3.3400755	-2.0951294
Pasture	14:p	-1.4113343	0.2396940	-1.8811346	-0.9415341

Appendix C. Beta Estimates for the Random Temporary Emigration Model at Three Survey Sites–Continued.

Population	Parameter	Beta	Standard Error	95% CI - Lower	95% CI - Upper
Pasture	15:p	-1.5582413	0.2759953	-2.0991920	-1.0172905
Pasture	16:p	-1.7601037	0.2995539	-2.3472293	-1.1729781
Pasture	17:p	-0.6475756	0.1854824	-1.0111210	-0.2840301
Pasture	18:p	-0.9166140	0.2551380	-1.4166846	-0.4165434
Pasture	19:p	-0.8658436	0.2989437	-1.4517733	-0.2799140
Pasture	20:p	-0.9967708	0.1913642	-1.3718446	-0.6216970
Pasture	21:p	-0.7051790	0.2624740	-1.2196281	-0.1907300
Pasture	22:p	-0.9908308	0.3000938	-1.5790148	-0.4026469
Pasture	23:p	-0.7897649	0.1733851	-1.1295996	-0.4499301
Pasture	24:p	-0.6775872	0.2526245	-1.1727313	-0.1824431
Pasture	25:p	-0.5636572	0.3125221	-1.1762005	0.0488861
Pasture	26:p	-0.9152583	0.1669051	-1.2423923	-0.5881243
Pasture	27:p	-0.9354982	0.2383651	-1.4026938	-0.4683027
Pasture	28:p	-0.8579827	0.2928604	-1.4319891	-0.2839764
Pasture	29:c offset	0.7533595	0.2683268	0.2274390	1.2792801
Warner's	1:	-1.508866	0.624072	-2.7320472	-0.2856847
Warner's	2:	1.0060822	1.7105928	-2.3466797	4.3588441
Warner's	3:	2.6322806	6.9566812	-11.002815	16.267376
Warner's	4:	0.7738575	1.4158111	-2.0011323	3.5488472
Warner's	5:	2.1179704	4.1650257	-6.0454802	10.281421
Warner's	6:	2.1702709	4.4850288	-6.6203857	10.960927
Warner's	7:	0.2652943	0.6927772	-1.092549	1.6231376
Warner's	8:	2.9577852	1.8387153	-0.6460968	6.5616672

Appendix C. Beta Estimates for the Random Temporary Emigration Model at Three Survey Sites– Continued.

Population	Parameter	Beta	Standard Error	95% CI - Lower	95% CI - Upper
Warner's	9:	-1.7545259	0.3088001	-2.3597741	-1.1492777
Warner's	10:	-2.404848	0.3448896	-3.0808315	-1.7288644
Warner's	11:	-1.6796207	0.3529593	-2.3714208	-0.9878205
Warner's	12:	-1.4296917	0.3800918	-2.1746717	-0.6847118
Warner's	13:	-1.0674952	0.3612713	-1.775587	-0.3594034
Warner's	14:	-0.8875394	0.3852467	-1.642623	-0.1324559
Warner's	15:	-1.2282439	0.4115328	-2.0348483	-0.4216396
Warner's	16:	-1.0889476	0.4278723	-1.9275774	-0.2503178
Warner's	17:	-1.9647471	0.3320296	-2.6155252	-1.313969
Warner's	18:	-0.3412545	0.2956812	-0.9207897	0.2382807
Warner's	19:	-1.0984445	0.3445621	-1.7737863	-0.4231028
Warner's	20:	-0.4694695	0.3917759	-1.2373503	0.2984113
Warner's	21:	-1.6152412	0.2788293	-2.1617466	-1.0687358
Warner's	22:	-1.264629	0.3173633	-1.886661	-0.642597
Warner's	23:	-1.9708374	0.3467273	-2.6504229	-1.2912519
Warner's	24:	-2.1247945	0.3607438	-2.8318523	-1.4177367
Warner's	25:	-0.9395568	0.2009018	-1.3333244	-0.5457892
Warner's	26:	-1.1186687	0.2640855	-1.6362763	-0.6010611
Warner's	27:	-0.7983038	0.3157074	-1.4170904	-0.1795171
Warner's	28:	-0.8517964	0.3528416	-1.543366	-0.1602268
Warner's	29:	-1.1627216	0.2178691	-1.589745	-0.7356981
Warner's	30:	-0.9562635	0.2774093	-1.4999857	-0.4125412
Warner's	31:	-1.5141647	0.313278	-2.1281896	-0.9001397

Appendix C. Beta Estimates for the Random Temporary Emigration Model at Three Survey Sites–Continued.

Population	Parameter	Beta	Standard Error	95% CI - Lower	95% CI - Upper
Warner's	32:	-0.9936229	0.3428201	-1.6655503	-0.3216955
Warner's	33:	-0.9251569	0.2659168	-1.4463538	-0.40396
Warner's	34:	-1.0723093	0.323445	-1.7062616	-0.4383571
Warner's	35:	-1.7226781	0.3404873	-2.3900332	-1.0553229
Warner's	36:	0.8286581	0.2974762	0.2456048	1.4117115

30